20 Ways your

Food & Drink Business can Survive BREXIT

20 Ways your Food & Drink Business can Survive BREXIT

by Brexit Info UK

© 2019 by Brexit info UK All rights reserved.

No part of this book may be reproduced in any written, electronic, recording, or photocopying form without written permission of the author, Brexit Info UK

Table of Contents
1. Introduction
2. Why should you prepare for Brexit?
3. Disruption
4. 5 Tips Before You Start Preparing
5. Food
6. Non-food Products
7. Security
8. Financial Crisis
9. The Withdrawal Agreement

INTRODUCTION

The one certainty about the UK's decision to leave the European Union is that it will trigger fundamental changes in the way organisations do business.

It is important that your business stays as flexible and focused as possible to meet any challenges which Brexit may bring. It is also time to look at the opportunities which Brexit presents for your business.

We recognise different businesses face different circumstances. Now is the time to reconsider and evaluate your business strategy so that you can adapt quickly to the new environment as it continues to evolve.

Everyone's (probably least) favourite subject right now is Brexit, and the potential effect it will have on the economy, immigration, and the country as a whole. What's harder to figure out though, is what that actually means for the average family household and business.

Regardless of whether you're a Leaver or a Remainer, deal or no deal, there are potential implications for most ordinary businesses.

This ebook is to explore a few things you might want to be aware of, that have possible implications for you and your business. It also includes some money tips, that will hopefully help with any potential financial changes as a result of Brexit.

WHY SHOULD YOU PREPARE FOR BREXIT

The aim of this guide is to provide information to help your business prepare for disruption when Briton leaves the EU.

Being prepared is not about hording masses of food and weapons in case of a zombie attack. Preparedness is about ensuring that you and your business are able to be self-sufficient in situations that could potentially happen.

Whether you voted leave or not, whether Briton leaves the EU with a deal or not, it's clear that no one is clear about how things will resolve. This guide is not "project fear". This guide will advise on how you can make provisions of your own, so that you are not dependant on government assistants should there be any disruption.

Briton leaving the EU is the biggest change that this country has had to manage in a lifetime. Government at all levels have been, and will continue to be, completely overwhelmed by the challenge of how to implement the result of the referendum. The government advice is that there may be disruption. Businesses have been advised to plan ahead. However there has been very little advice for industries. Should there be any disruption that affects, food, day to day products, utilities – the government is completely unprepared to support you.

It has been a surprise to many just how dependant some sectors are on "just in time" production lines. Most people live week to week and pay cheque to pay cheque. We are used to going to our local shop and buying what ever we want, when ever we want. It is difficult and destressing to imagine that we might not be able to do that with such ease for a few weeks or even months. If there is any disruption that affects food there is likely to be mass panic. That is why it is so important that you make sensible preparations for your own business now.

Disruption

How long should you prepare for?

If the UK leaves the EU with a deal there is likely to be minimal disruption. However, even with a deal independent research studies have stated that the government has left it too late to implement the changes necessary.

If the UK leaves the EU without a deal, opinion ranges from minimal disruption to significant disruption. The government advice is that businesses should prepare for 3 – 6 months of disruption.

If there is going to be significant disruption it is likely to be at its most severe within the first 2 – 6 weeks after Briton leaves the EU. It would be difficult for most people to prepare for 6 months. However, it is a good idea to keep in the back of your mind that at worse case scenario it could take six months or more for systems to be implemented.

What kind of disruption could there be and how will it affect me?

- Food and product shortages

Delays in food and products getting through the border is a concern that most people have. It has been well reported that a few minutes of checks added on to each lorry could potentially course significant delays. Supermarkets have warned that they are unable to stock pile fresh food. If there are delays, we could start seeing gaps on our shelves within two weeks.

- Civil unrest or an increase in crime

Civil unrest could be sparked by a number of things. Mass protest for or against Brexit could turn into unrest. The most likely course of civil unrest would be any shortage of food in our stores.

- Blackouts

Some areas of the UK, for example Northern Ireland are at a high risk of experiencing blackouts.

- Petrol

This is unlikely, however if there is disruption it could have a wider affecting the delivery of petrol to petrol stations.

- Water

There is a concern that the chemicals that are used to treat our water comes in from Europe. It would be a priority for the UK government to ensure that there is no risk to the quality of the UK drinking water.

5 TIPS TO PREPARE FOR BREXIT

1. Understand the consequences of Brexit

The impact of Brexit depends on the individual conditions of each company, the company's product, service, business model and activities in the British market in general. After Brexit, EU regulations may not apply in the British market and British regulations may not be accepted in the single market. Be aware that the company's British certificates, licenses and authorisations may no longer be valid in the EU post-Brexit. Also be aware that the responsibility of the company in the supply chain, stipulated in EU product rules, may change after Brexit.

2. Acquaint yourself with customs duty rules

Trade with the UK will be more difficult post-Brexit because it will be a third country. Depending on what kinds of goods the company trades, customs may apply, and it is necessary to prepare for customs procedures and new VAT procedures. If you have British customers or suppliers, acquaint yourself with the customs rules that will apply post-Brexit – particularly you have little or no experience in trading with third countries.

3. Consider your employees

Because free movement of labour between the UK and EU will become more limited after Brexit, it is important to consider how this will impact your business model and recruitment plans. Examine whether and how employees in the UK will be affected by visa restrictions and new residency rules in the UK.

4. Stay informed and use your network

Use official guides to stay informed. The EU Commission, British authorities and Danish ministries offer guides for companies about what to be aware of in a no-deal situation. Also use your own network to better assess how to handle Brexit in your company. Keep an eye on the activities of your clients, suppliers and partners in order to better predict how your own company may be affected.

5. Imports and the Exchange Rate

From cucumbers to computers, 17% of the money we spend is on imported goods. So whilst import prices and tariffs might seem far removed from us personally, they actually directly impact on not only our bigger purchases, but also our everyday buys.

The most immediate effect of the Brexit referendum, is the impact on the exchange rate. There was a depreciation in value of the pound by 13% between Jan 2016 – March 2017. It is uncertain whether Sterling is likely to depreciate further following Brexit, but as imported goods are purchased in the foreign currency, the exchange rate does directly impact of the cost of imported goods. Therefore, the lower the value of Sterling in the exchange rate, the more Sterling is needed to purchase the same amount of foreign currency which consequently means an increase in the cost of purchasing imports.

6. FOOD

Brexit, for better or worse, means a major structural change in how people in the UK think about the food they eat. There is an opportunity to reformulate food policy for the better, but this could be easily squandered if not managed carefully.

- For almost half a century, the UK's food system – comprising the totality of food production, transport, manufacturing, retailing and consumption – has been intrinsically and intricately linked to its membership of the European Community and, subsequently, the EU. Arguably, for no other sectors are the challenges and opportunities of Brexit as extensive as they are for UK food and agriculture.

- Reforming the UK's food system won't be easy. The 21st century economic, market, regulatory and political systems are exceedingly resistant to change, locked into the way they have evolved over decades. The tight Brexit timeline, the complexities of negotiations and the political pressure to secure new trade deals could easily lead to hasty decisions that are poorly conceived and become near impossible to correct.

7. Regulatory System

- There is a risk of a two-tier regulatory system emerging whereby, after its withdrawal from the EU, the UK produces food at higher standards but imports cheaper and potentially lower-quality food from countries with reduced welfare or environmental standards. These developments could affect consumer confidence and cause public distrust.
- Meanwhile, new market conditions could incentivize greater intensification and/or reduce the number of small farms,

affecting the profitability and structure of the UK farming sector. This should be managed carefully to ensure that the cultural link between British citizens and their rural environment is not negatively affected.

8. Supply Chains

- The UK will also need to invest in more reliable supply chains and develop resilience in prospective partner countries to help them respond to the combined threats of climate change and global environmental degradation, as this could impact the resilience of the UK's food system, food prices and availability.

- Currently, the UK operates on a 'just in time' food system, maintaining five to 10 days' worth of groceries in the country (often less in the case of fresh produce). Once the UK is outside the EU, its food industry will need to factor in time for longer inspections of food imports at its borders, and build the necessary infrastructure to conduct these checks.

- The UK has an unprecedented opportunity, in the context of Brexit, to equip its food system to withstand these challenges, but the transition will need to be managed carefully. Any reconfiguration will first need to understand and take account of what citizens and consumers value most about the food system. Second, a UK-wide and cross-government approach will be necessary to foster a holistic, profitable, healthy and sustainable food system for all. Processing, supply chains and labelling must be transparent, and must take full advantage of new technologies available.

9. Food Prices

- A not insignificant 30% of the food we buy is imported, with 70% of that currently imported from the EU. This means that changes in tariffs and exchange rates for imports are likely to affect food prices for households in general.

- To get an idea of how depreciation of Sterling can affect the price that ordinary consumers like ourselves pay for food, we can look at previous history. In 2007 - 2008, there was a 21% depreciation. In this same period, the price of food increased by 8.7%. Although it is too soon to gauge whether the more recent depreciation will have a similar correlation with an increase in food prices, there is already some evidence to suggest that it might.

- Changes to the exchange rate along with the as yet undecided changes in tariffs, will directly affect how much it costs for imported goods to reach our supermarkets. This in turn will affect the prices we pay as consumers.

10. NON-FOOD PRODUCTS

Under a "no deal" Brexit scenario, where all imported goods from the EU were subject to World Trade Organization tariffs, the overall cost to households would be £27bn a year, or nearly £1,000 per household.

"In a scenario where the UK reverted to WTO most-favoured-nation import tariffs, we expect the price of a typical weekly grocery shop to go up by £5.50, a family meal for four at a high street restaurant chain to increase by £9, and a pair of trainers to cost £6.75 more," said Duncan Brewer, Oliver Wyman partner and author of the research.

11. Household costs to increase

The research modelled five of the most commonly discussed scenarios of an UK exit from the EU: a deal that left the UK out of the customs union but in the single market, and vice versa; one in which the UK achieved a bespoke customs and single market deal; and two in which the UK left the single market and customs union but, in one alternative, applied WTO tariffs to imports and, in the other, unilaterally decided to apply zero tariffs to imports.

It found that the annual average increase to household costs under the scenarios ranged from £245 to £961 annually. It also found that, for each 5 per cent that sterling devalued against the US dollar and the euro, household costs increased by a further £380 a year.

Any subsequent free trade deals, which allowed the UK to move to zero-tariff trade with all non-EU countries, would reduce costs by £120 to £170.

According to the research, worse-off households would see costs rise more than richer ones because they spend a higher proportion of their income after housing costs on groceries.

12. Loo roll shortages

One of the surprising, but vital, items that could be at risk, if there were delays in transporting goods, is toilet roll. According to former Labour MP and Minister for Europe Denis MacShane, the UK is the biggest importer of loo paper in the whole of Europe and it only stocks one day's worth of supply. This means that a delay of a day or more could see shops facing shortages.

13. Security

Crime might increase for a number of reasons after the UK Leaves the EU:
1. Food shortages can course people to panic, riot, be violent and/or turn to crime.
2. Civil unrest in protest for or against Brexit.
3. A shortage of medication might affect people that are drug misuses to committee more crime.
4. Criminals may try and take advantage of how stretched police forces are.

Should security become a concern for you and your business the aim is:
- Deter

Aim to deter criminals with good lighting around your business. Invest in security lights that can be a very effective deterrent. Door alarms, business alarms and security cameras are also a good idea to consider.

Q. How would I defend my business if a mob is at my front door?

A. Ultimately nothing is worth your life or taking somebody else's life. Prevention is the aim here. So, ensure that you have strong doors and locks and goods are well hidden out of sight. As in the 2011 London riots the police were completely over stretched so would not be able to come to your aid. If it was just you under attack it might be best to flee with what you can. People that are hungry and rioting do stupid things. If people are rioting outside your door you need to have a plan to escape not confront or defend.

14. FINANCIAL CRISIS

A Black Friday

Call it a black Friday or what you will, the events that unfolded on the 24th of June 2016 would remain an enigma in the minds of the millions who voted and those across the Globe who watched in awe as history was rewritten 43 years after Britain was officially signed in as a part of the Eurozone. Almost immediately after the landmark outcome of the referendum came to light, markets around the globe reacted wildly even as the Pound Sterling suffered its biggest single day fall ever. While investors rushed to find solace in Bonds and Gold, the strength of the Japanese Yen forced investors out of equity markets across the Eurozone and beyond.

After the UK leaves the EU most economic forecasters believe that the UK, in the short to medium term, will need to adjust. This may mean that we still grow, but not as fast as we would if we were still in the EU. Or it may mean that UK growth slows down or we could go into recession. The severity of any recession is again a guessing game.

The Italian economy is now in recession and the German economy has slowed down considerably. When making your own assessment consider how resilient you believe the UK will be to weather a possible recession in the euro zone and a slowdown in the global economy.

The UK last went into recession over ten years ago, most economies go into recession every 8 to 10 years. The trade tensions between the USA and China is ongoing. The last financial crisis showed how intertwined countries' economies are. Should there be another financial crisis in the euro zone, America or China, the UK will be vulnerable.

Financial crisis is not imminent, but take these steps to over the next 24 months:

15. Reduce debt
16. Pay extra on you mortgage
17. Have an emergency fund – 3 to 6 months minimum
18. Have more than one income stream
19. Save

Q. What would I do if the government suddenly put limits on how much could be withdrawn from the bank each day?

A. During an economic crisis this is one option that the government could take. It happened in Grease. It is there for important to keep a small amount of cash at home. Keep your cupboards well stocked of food, and always have an extra week or two of non-perishable goods.

20. The Withdrawal Agreement

As the Brexit deadline looms, the exact terms of the UK's departure from the European Union remain alarmingly unclear — and if the chaos in parliament is anything to go by, a resolution isn't likely any time soon. Both sides of the Brexit negotiations – but, let's face it, mainly the British – celebrated getting past the European Union's March summit milestone broadly on schedule. Most of the separation issues are sorted out, there's a 21-month transition period agreed to in principle and the EU has issued its guidelines for the post-transition relationship. Sighs of relief all around.

Yet one look at the to-do list for between now and the EU's October deadline to conclude the talks reveals little room for complacency. As Peter Ptassek, Germany's Brexit coordinator, said on Twitter recently, there's been a "strange silence" from the U.K. since the summit breakthrough. "Not the right moment to talk?" he wondered. "EU awaiting U.K. response..." No date has yet been set for the next round of negotiations. Despite a huge gulf in the visions for the post-2020 relationship between the two sides, there has been little in the way of serious conversation between London and Brussels on how to bridge that divide.

While negotiators are at least in touch over how to solve the tricky issue of keeping the Irish border invisible after Brexit (the fourth in a series of U.K.-EU meetings on the topic takes place in Brussels today, with a session focusing on the rights of individuals), that's only one of a number of topics left over from the first phase of the negotiations. The draft 120-page Brexit treaty shows that, in addition to the Irish border, there's no agreement between the U.K. and EU yet on topics including:

governance of the Brexit deal, and what to do if there are disputes;

the power of the European Court of Justice over the U.K. before the end of the transition period, including the right to start new proceedings against Britain;

the ownership of nuclear material;

intellectual property registration;

ongoing police cooperation and sharing of law-enforcement information;

cooperation in civil law and commercial matters.

That treaty, which must be approved by the British and European parliaments and a weighted majority of 72 percent of the remaining EU member states before Brexit day next March, will sit alongside what the EU calls a "political declaration" about the future. Any agreement about future trade will be in that declaration and referred to in the treaty. But it won't be legally binding and probably will fall a long way short of the fully fledged trade deal that the U.K. hopes to have ready for the end of the transition period. How detailed the declaration will be depends on the amount of work that can be done over the next six months and the willingness – or otherwise – of both sides to make concrete commitments now about the future.

www.ingramcontent.com/pod-product-compliance
Lightning Source LLC
Chambersburg PA
CBHW030549220526
45463CB00007B/3036